What Was
the Underground Railroad?

by Yona Zeldis McDonough

illustrated by Lauren Mortimer

Grosset & Dunlap
An Imprint of Penguin Group (USA) LLC

For Jane O'Connor, guiding light
and shining star—YZM

For Jade, my pea in a pod.
There is no better friend than a twin sister. And
there is no better twin sister than you—LM

GROSSET & DUNLAP
Published by the Penguin Group
Penguin Group (USA) LLC
375 Hudson Street
New York, New York 10014, USA

USA | Canada | UK | Ireland | Australia | New Zealand | India | South Africa | China

penguin.com
A Penguin Random House Company

Text copyright © 2013 by Yona Zeldis McDonough. Illustrations copyright © 2013 by Penguin Group (USA) LLC. All rights reserved. Published by Grosset & Dunlap, a division of Penguin Young Readers Group, 345 Hudson Street, New York, New York 10014. GROSSET & DUNLAP is a trademark of Penguin Group (USA) LLC. Printed in the U.S.A.

Library of Congress Cataloging-in-Publication Data is available.

ISBN 978-0-448-46712-2   10 9

Contents

What Was the Underground Railroad?

On a March day in 1849, two men tossed a big wooden box onto a steamboat that was about to head up the Potomac River to Washington, DC. Nobody cared how the box landed. The men thought that it was just filled with something ordinary. But they were wrong. Inside the box was a real, live man. His name was Henry Brown.

He was a slave escaping from Virginia. He was hoping to reach Philadelphia, Pennsylvania. Slavery was illegal in Pennsylvania. He would be free there—as long as slave catchers didn't find him and bring him back to the South.

The box with Henry in it landed upside down. Now he was on his head! He was scared and, oh, how his head hurt! Would he ever get to Philadelphia? He didn't know.

Although he was on a steamship, Henry was traveling on something called the Underground Railroad. The Underground Railroad was not an actual railroad, with metal tracks and passenger cars. And it did not run underground. No one knows for sure where the name came from. It meant the escape route African American slaves took to reach freedom.

One story says that in 1831, a slave named Tice Davids fled from Kentucky to Ohio. Kentucky was a slave state. Ohio was a free state.

When Davids's master found out, he was shocked. It was as if Tice Davids had vanished into thin air. The master joked that his slave "must have gone off on an underground railroad." Is this story true? No one knows for sure. But the term Underground Railroad stuck.

Escaped slaves fled to free states and Canada any way they could. They often went on foot, traveling hundreds of miles. They went hidden in wagons. They went by train and by boat. They often went at night, to avoid capture. Whites and other blacks along the way helped them. These people were called *conductors*.

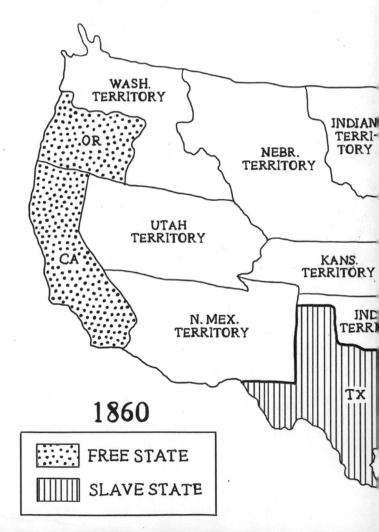

1860

FREE STATE

SLAVE STATE

The journeys were scary and filled with danger. If caught, the slaves would be sent back and severely punished. But the danger did not stop them. Freedom was worth the risk. This is the story of some of these people, who they were, where they went, what happened to them along the way, and how their lives changed.

CHAPTER 1
The Slave Trade

In 1619, a ship docked in Jamestown, Virginia. It carried about twenty people who had been kidnapped from their homes in West Africa. These were the very first slaves brought to America.

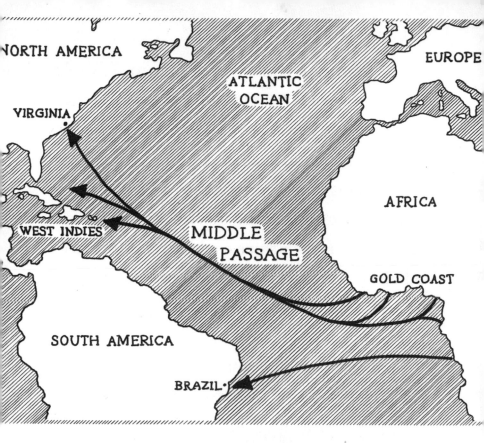

By 1860, there were nearly four million slaves in the United States. Virginia and other states in the South depended on the free labor of slaves to work the fields on farms called plantations. Every year brought more slaves. They arrived on slave ships. The trip from Africa across the Atlantic Ocean was known as the Middle Passage.

The journey typically lasted four to six weeks. However, it could take as long as twelve weeks. Even a short trip was awful. There were two ways for the captains to load their ships with slaves: loose packing and tight packing.

Loose packing meant captains didn't take as many slaves as their ships could carry. More space and air for the slaves on board made it less likely that they would become sick and die. Healthy slaves brought a better price.

Tight packing was much worse. The captain would crowd as many slaves into the ship as

possible. Slaves were packed like sardines in spaces that were sometimes no more than eighteen inches high. There was barely room to move or even breathe. The captain didn't care. He figured that the more slaves on board, the more money he would make in America. If some slaves died, so what?

What was it like on a slave ship? Slaves were often chained ankle to wrist. There were no bathrooms. The slaves used buckets instead. With no way to keep their living spaces clean, slaves came down with diseases like the flu and smallpox.

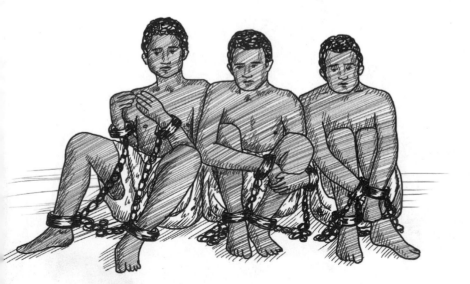

To save money, some captains brought along very little food. As a result, many slaves starved to death. The Middle Passage was so horrible, some slaves preferred to jump overboard and drown. Or they simply stopped eating.

If they survived the journey to America, slaves were sold in auctions. This meant that white people bid money to buy them, just like they might buy a horse or a cow. Each slave was sold to the person who bid the highest price.

Auctions were advertised with signs and in newspapers. At an auction, a large group of newly arrived black men, women, and children were put on display. White people came beforehand to inspect the slaves. They pried open their mouths to check their teeth. They pinched their muscles to measure their strength. No one cared about how the slaves felt. They were not considered human beings.

Auctions tore families apart. After a mother was sold, she might have to watch one of her children get sold to an owner from a different state. Her baby would be yanked away from her, and there was nothing she could do about it. Husbands and wives, fathers and mothers, sisters and brothers were often sent to live on plantations far away from each other. In most cases, they never saw each other again.

In 1808, the United States ended the slave trade. No more slaves could be brought to America. But the law didn't change anything for the slaves already in the United States. They were still slaves. And their children and grandchildren would be born slaves. So the number of slaves in America grew and grew. The only hope for a better life for these African Americans was to escape.

CHAPTER 2
Life on a Plantation

Slavery took root in the Southern states because there was so much good farmland. Big plantations needed lots of workers to tend the crops. And slaves had to work for free. In the 1600s, many plantations grew tobacco. In the 1700s, the big

crops in the South were rice and indigo. In the 1800s, the main crop was cotton.

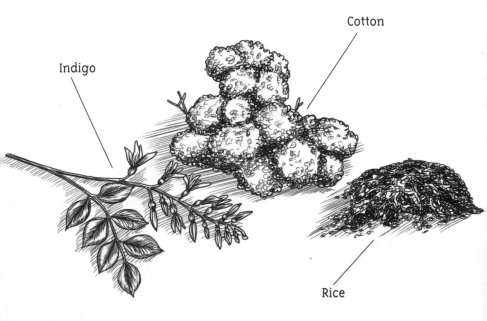

Indigo

Cotton

Rice

First the slaves had to pluck little balls of cotton from the cotton plants. Next they had to clean the cotton balls and get them ready for spinning. Then the cotton was spun and turned into cloth.

The richest slave owners lived on big estates and might own as many as four hundred slaves.

These slave owners lived like lords and ladies. They had fancy parties and dances. They went on hunts. They ate good food and wore expensive clothes. There were small plantations, too. They were more like ordinary farms. The owners weren't rich and might own only a couple of slaves. But slave labor supported all the plantations, large and small.

Slaves did not live like their masters. Their life was mostly work, work, and more work. If they did something wrong, they were often beaten or whipped. Slave children did not go to school. In fact, slaves were forbidden to learn how to read or write. They could not vote or own a home. They couldn't own anything.

Some slaves worked in the fields. A field slave worked from sunrise to sunset. Women worked as hard as men. Pregnant women worked in the fields right up until the birth of their babies. Then they worked with their babies strapped to their backs. Children over the age of twelve were expected to work as hard as adults.

The field slaves were watched all day long by an overseer with a whip. The overseer was usually a white man. He made sure the slaves never wasted a moment. If they did, a flick of the whip made them get back to work. Field slaves usually lived in tiny huts with dirt floors. In winter, the huts were freezing cold. Instead of beds, they had only rough blankets and maybe some straw.

At the end of the long day in the fields, slaves on a cotton plantation had to line up. Their cotton was weighed. They were expected to pick at least two hundred pounds of cotton a day.

Field slaves had Sundays off. Sometimes they

were given Saturday afternoon off, too. But not
during harvest time. Then, they might work an
eighteen-hour day.

House slaves worked mostly indoors. They cleaned, cooked, served meals, and took care of the master's children. They waited on tables, washed, ironed, swept, dusted, hoed, and weeded gardens. House slaves also did weaving, mending, quilting, and spinning. Some slaves learned to make lace.

House slaves often lived in closets or corners of the Big House, even if the rest of their families

lived in the slave quarters. Although they did not get Sundays off, most house slaves lived better than field slaves. House slaves sometimes even managed to learn how to read and write.

But field or house, inside or out, one thing was certain: Life as a slave was a nightmare. The dream of every slave was to be free.

CHAPTER 3
Abolition

At one point, slavery existed in every part of the United States. Even the North. In fact, Founding Father Benjamin Franklin owned a few slaves for many years, until he came to see slavery as evil. All the thirteen original colonies allowed slavery. However, over time, slavery died out in the North. By 1804, it was outlawed in Vermont, Pennsylvania, Massachusetts, New Hampshire, Connecticut, Rhode Island, New York, and New Jersey.

When the Northwest Territory was created in 1787, slavery was not allowed there. So all the states created from that territory were free states: Ohio, Indiana, Illinois, Michigan, Wisconsin, and Minnesota. In addition, Iowa, Maine, California,

Oregon, and Kansas were all admitted before the Civil War as free states.

In 1861, when the Civil War broke out, there were nineteen free states and fifteen slave states. There were also eight free territories, which were areas not yet officially made states.

Why was it so different in the North?

People living in the Northern states didn't need large numbers of farm workers the way people in the South did. Most farms in the North were small, because the land wasn't very good for growing crops. More and more people became shopkeepers, craftsmen, factory workers, and merchants.

From the moment the United States was born, there were people who believed that slavery was just plain wrong. They wanted it to end. Some could accept slavery ending slowly over time. But some people wanted to end—or abolish—slavery right away. These people were called abolitionists.

Which Presidents Owned Slaves?

Twelve US presidents owned slaves. Here are the ones who did. Eight of them owned slaves while in office.

Four others owned slaves at some point in their lives.

George
Washington

Andrew Johnson

Martin Van Buren

Ulysses S. Grant

William Henry
Harrison

William Lloyd Garrison was a leader in the American abolitionist movement. Garrison was a poor boy from Massachusetts. He first worked as a printer and then went on to become a writer and editor. In 1831, he published the first issue of a newspaper called the *Liberator*. In its pages, he called for an immediate end to slavery. Garrison was known and admired for his firm beliefs and his fiery way of expressing them.

With Arthur Tappan and others, Garrison founded the American Anti-Slavery Society. The society was started in 1833. By 1838, it had 1,350 local chapters and 250,000 members. Some were former slaves, such as Frederick Douglass and William Wells Brown. They gave speeches to bring other people to their cause. The headquarters of the society was in New York City, and from 1840 to 1870, it published a weekly newspaper. It was called the *National Anti-Slavery Standard.*

Many abolitionists in the United States were Quakers. Started in England in 1648, the Quakers were a Christian group who believed that people should tremble at the word of the Lord. That's where the name "Quakers" came from. Quakers wore plain clothes and led simple lives. They did not own many things. There are still Quakers today. They worship in Quaker meetinghouses, without ministers. Instead, each member of the group is allowed to speak. Equality is an important part of the Quaker religion. For that reason, Quakers like John Woolman (from New Jersey) and Thomas Garrett (from Pennsylvania) were early outspoken critics of slavery.

Slavery did not end for good until 1865, at the end of the Civil War. Up until then, many abolitionists took part in the Underground Railroad. Some became conductors who helped runaway slaves escape. Their homes, stores, stables, and barns were used as safe stations on

the Underground Railroad, places where slaves could hide. John Fairfield, who was from a slave-holding family, became a famous conductor. Unlike the peace-loving Quakers, Fairfield carried a gun. He helped hundreds of slaves escape, often by pretending to be a slave owner himself.

Even though they put themselves at risk, the conductors on the Underground Railroad did so to help people who were not free.

CHAPTER 4
A Path to Freedom

In the 1820s, a white man named John Rankin moved from the slave state of Tennessee to the free state of Ohio. He bought a house in a town on the Ohio River. Every night, John Rankin raised a lantern to the top of a pole in his front yard. Why did he keep doing this?

Slaves fleeing from Tennessee had to cross the Ohio River, and John Rankin wanted to help them. The lantern showed the way to the river. The lantern was a beacon and a guide. It also was a sign that Rankin's home was a safe house. Slaves could stop there and get food, shelter, and clothing before heading off again.

John Rankin became famous for helping slaves escape. Plantation owners were furious with him. Some came across the river and attacked his house. They even tried to set it on fire. But that did not stop Rankin. He continued to help runaways until slavery was finally outlawed.

Around the same time, a Quaker named Levi Coffin lived in Newport, Indiana. Indiana was a free state that shared a border with Kentucky, a slave state. Even in Indiana, however, many people didn't see anything wrong with slavery.

Coffin and his wife, Catherine, however, hated slavery. If they could help slaves fleeing from Kentucky, of course they would. Not only did the Coffins feed and clothe the runaways, sometimes Levi Coffin took them to a house farther north.

Coffin had a special wagon with a secret compartment in the bottom. This compartment could hide a slave or two. Sometimes he hid them under bales of hay, or in boxes.

In the early 1820s, most people like John Rankin and the Coffins worked alone. They were not part of any group. But by around 1830, abolitionists began to see themselves as part of a team. They began to work together. A new language was developed. They called their homes or other stopping places *stations*. They called themselves *stationmasters*, *conductors*, or *operators*. Travel routes were called *lines*. And they called the escaping slaves *cargo* or *passengers* on this unusual train to freedom.

News of the railroad spread south. Slaves who made it to freedom in the North might become conductors. Free blacks living in the North became conductors, too. All these people helped the Underground Railroad to grow. By the 1840s, there was a system in place.

But because it was a secret, no records were kept. Even today, we don't know exactly how the Underground Railroad operated. We do know that networks were set up in Illinois, Indiana, Ohio, Pennsylvania, New York, New Jersey, and the states in New England.

Slaves escaping from Gulf states such as Louisiana, Mississippi, and Alabama typically went north to Illinois, Wisconsin, and Michigan. Slaves from the East Coast usually went to Pennsylvania, New York, Connecticut, and Maine. Slaves in Texas went in the opposite direction, south to Mexico. Mexico was a country where slavery was illegal.

Routes to Freedom

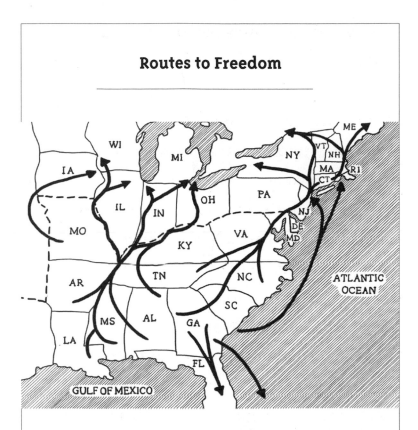

Slaves took many routes to freedom. Slaves who lived in North Carolina or Virginia tried to get to New York City, Philadelphia, or Boston. Those from Mississippi went to Cleveland, Detroit, or Chicago. Not all slaves went north. Slaves in Georgia might escape to the Everglades, Cuba, Jamaica, or Haiti.

Often slaves picked winter, around Christmas, to escape. They had time off for the holiday. So it might take several days before they were missed. Also, in winter the Ohio River would be frozen and easier to get across. (Escape routes often involved crossing the Ohio River.)

Slaves found secret ways to let their friends know of their plans to escape. They often sang while they worked in the fields. Their overseers did not pay attention to the words of the songs. One song called "Let My People Go" let other slaves know that the singer was about to run away.

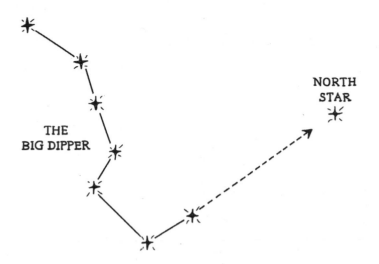

Slaves used hollowed-out gourds as water dippers. But a drinking gourd was also a code word for the Big Dipper, the constellation that points to the North Star. Runaway slaves needed to follow the North Star to escape to freedom. So following the drinking gourd was a phrase that also meant slaves were going to try and run away.

Slave owners didn't like to talk about the North. They didn't want slaves to know they could find a better life there. Often masters made up lies. They said black people were treated terribly up North, worse than on plantations. That did not keep slaves from running away. Slave owners also said it was too cold to live in Canada. One male slave said, "We knew Canada was a good country for us because master was so anxious that we *not* go there."

On their journey to freedom, slaves took nothing with them, just themselves. They had to stay on the run, even when they did not know where their next step would lead them.

Because most slaves didn't know how to read, many didn't even understand where exactly the North was or how to get there. The only thing they knew was that "North" meant no slavery. And that was enough.

On the road, slaves looked out for lanterns or quilts hung over the porches. A colorful quilt displayed outdoors might be another sign of a safe house. Because of all the time spent in hiding, it might take slaves weeks or months to travel a short distance that normally took only a few days.

They had to survive on very little sleep and food. Worst of all was the fear.

Here is how a runaway slave named Josiah Henson described it: "A fearful dread of detection ever pursued me. I would start out of my sleep in terror, my heart beating against my ribs, and expecting to find dogs and slave hunters after me."

Slave Catchers

From Georgia all the way up to Michigan, slave catchers combed roads, docks, and city streets looking for escaped slaves. Many took along trained bloodhounds. Sometimes, a slave catcher would arrest the wrong person, such as a free black man or woman. The slave catcher did not care. He just wanted to collect a reward. Slave catchers might earn as much as $600 a year hunting down escaped slaves. That was a lot of money back then.

Henson was right to be afraid. Runaway slaves were hunted down and often captured. Bloodhounds sniffed out runaways that were still in nearby woods or swamps. For slaves that managed to get farther away, a plantation owner might hire a slave catcher. These men earned money by capturing escaped slaves and returning them to their masters. They patrolled docks and train stations, looking for runaways.

If caught, an escaped slave would be severely punished. When a slave named George Tinsley tried to escape, he was chased by dogs that tore off his clothes and bit him. Then he was put in the pillory, a big piece of timber with a hole for his head, and whipped.

Conductors on the Underground Railroad were punished, too. In 1848, Thomas Garrett

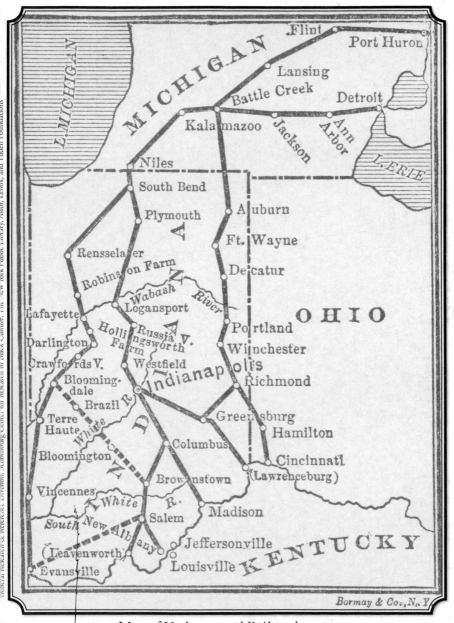

Map of Underground Railroad routes
through Indiana, Ohio, and Michigan

Ohio abolitionists John and Jane Rankin

Wood engraving
depicting a slave
auction in
Richmond, Virginia

Receipt from 1840 for a $250 payment for a male slave

Relics of Slavery Days

Slave quarters at the Hermitage Plantation
outside of Savannah, Georgia

Poster advertising an "Anti-
Slave-Catchers' Convention"
in Milwaukee, Wisconsin, on
April 13, 1854

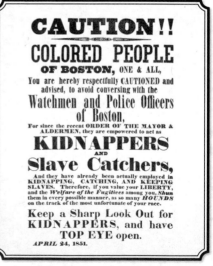

An 1851 poster warning
African Americans about the
Fugitive Slave Law

A photo featuring five generations of a slave family
on a plantation in Beaufort, South Carolina

A 1910 photo of Uncle "Billy" Marshall, an African American
conductor on the Underground Railroad from Ripley, Ohio

Portrait of Ellen Craft wearing the
disguise she used to escape from slavery

An image circa 1875–1880 of African American
workers amid bales of cotton

Nineteenth-century painting that shows
African Americans escaping from slavery

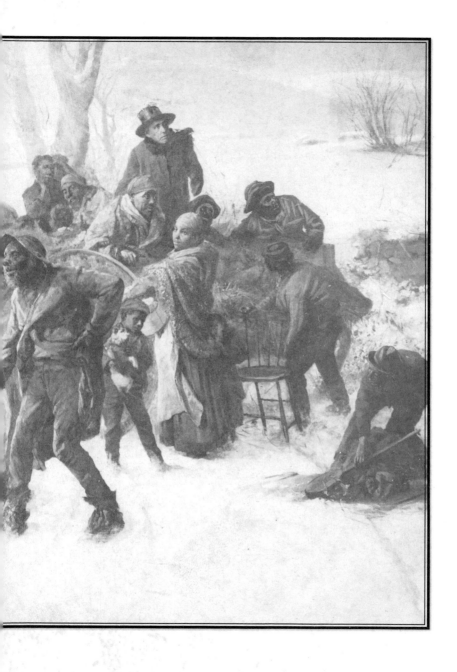

Harriet Tubman (1823 – 1913)
nurse, spy and scout

Harriet Tubman

Sojourner Truth, a former slave
and abolitionist leader, in 1864

Frederick Douglass in 1856

Emancipated slaves working for the US Army in Virginia

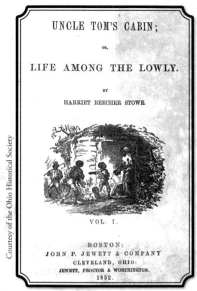

Title page of the first edition of
Harriet Beecher Stowe's 1852
antislavery novel,
Uncle Tom's Cabin

Oil portrait from 1855 of
William Lloyd Garrison,
founding editor of the
abolitionist newspaper
The Liberator

Copy of *The Liberator*, dated
December 21, 1833

Lithograph from 1850 depicting Frederick Douglass and others as they watch Henry "Box" Brown emerge from a crate

Caroline Quarlls Watkins when she lived in Sandwich, Ontario

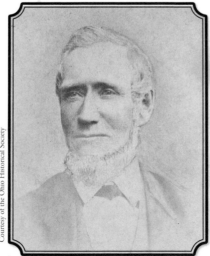

Underground Railroad operator George P. Clark

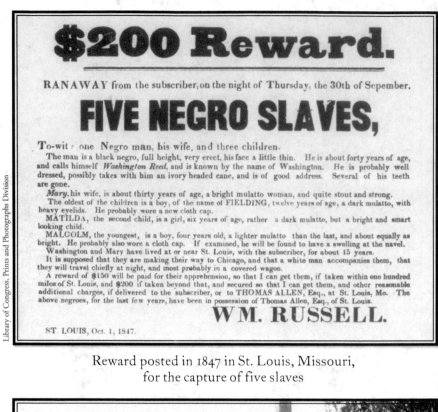

$200 Reward.

RANAWAY from the subscriber, on the night of Thursday, the 30th of Sepember.

FIVE NEGRO SLAVES,

To-wit : one Negro man, his wife, and three children.

The man is a black negro, full height, very erect, his face a little thin. He is about forty years of age, and calls himself *Washington Reed*, and is known by the name of Washington. He is probably well dressed, possibly takes with him an ivory headed cane, and is of good address. Several of his teeth are gone.

Mary, his wife, is about thirty years of age, a bright mulatto woman, and quite stout and strong.

The oldest of the children is a boy, of the name of FIELDING, twelve years of age, a dark mulatto, with heavy eyelids. He probably wore a new cloth cap.

MATILDA, the second child, is a girl, six years of age, rather a dark mulatto, but a bright and smart looking child.

MALCOLM, the youngest, is a boy, four years old, a lighter mulatto than the last, and about equally as bright. He probably also wore a cloth cap. If examined, he will be found to have a swelling at the navel. Washington and Mary have lived at or near St. Louis, with the subscriber, for about 15 years.

It is supposed that they are making their way to Chicago, and that a white man accompanies them, that they will travel chiefly at night, and most probably in a covered wagon.

A reward of $150 will be paid for their apprehension, so that I can get them, if taken within one hundred miles of St. Louis, and $200 if taken beyond that, and secured so that I can get them, and other reasonable additional charges, if delivered to the subscriber, or to THOMAS ALLEN, Esq., at St. Louis, Mo. The above negroes, for the last few years, have been in possession of Thomas Allen, Esq., of St. Louis.

WM. RUSSELL.

ST. LOUIS, Oct. 1, 1847.

Reward posted in 1847 in St. Louis, Missouri,
for the capture of five slaves

The raising of a lantern on the flagpole in
Ripley, Ohio, used to signal to fugitive slaves

Thomas L. Gray in front of his house in Deavertown, Ohio,
which served as a station on the Underground Railroad

The Magee House in Canisteo, New York,
which was an Underground Railroad station

Wood engraving depicting African Americans
in Washington, DC, on April 19, 1866, celebrating
the end of slavery

EMANCIPATED SLAVES BROUGHT FROM LOUISIANA BY COL. GEORGE H. HANKS.

The Children are from the Schools established by order of Maj. Gen. Banks.

A photo from 1863 of slaves who found freedom in the North

was fined about $5,400 for hiding escaping slaves in Wilmington, Delaware. That was a lot of money back then. Garrett lost his home and nearly everything else, too.

In 1844, a sea captain named Jonathan Walker was caught helping eight slaves escape by boat from Pensacola, Florida. A red-hot iron was pressed into Walker's palm. He was branded with the letters *SS*, for "slave stealer." Samuel A. Smith, a white man who helped three slaves escape from Virginia, was sent to jail for eight years. In the free states, anyone caught helping or harboring a runaway slave could be fined $1,000.

Despite the many dangers for both passengers and conductors, as many as 2,500 slaves a year "rode" to freedom between 1830 and 1860. The most famous conductor on the Underground Railroad was a former slave named Harriet Tubman. She was so brave and heroic that she deserves a chapter of her own.

CHAPTER 5
The Great Conductor

Harriet Ross Tubman was born in Maryland around 1820. Her parents could not read or write, so they could not record the exact date of her birth. She was originally called Araminta or "Minty," the fifth of the nine children born to Harriet "Rit" Green and Benjamin Ross.

Edward Brodas was their master. When Minty was just a little girl, Brodas hired her out to another family. Minty had to watch the baby at night. If the baby cried, Minty got a whipping. She had to sleep on the floor. There was no mattress or blanket. To stay warm, she buried her feet in the ashes by the fire. One time Minty stole a sugar cube from the table. She had never tasted sugar before and could not resist. Then she hid in a pigpen to put off the whipping she knew would follow.

When she was a young girl, Minty worked as a field hand. She liked being outside better than she liked being indoors. Once an overseer threw an iron weight at another slave, but it hit Minty in the head instead.

Minty recovered, but she suffered from headaches and sleeping spells for the rest of her life.

Around 1844, she married a local free black named John Tubman. It was then that she started calling herself Harriet, like her mother.

In 1849, Mr. Brodas died. Harriet heard rumors that she was going to be sold. Fearing the worst, she decided to escape and go north. She wanted John to go with her, but he said no. So Harriet went by herself. Packing a little salt pork, some corn bread, and a quilt she had sewn, she set out at night. She was given shelter in the home of a Quaker woman in Maryland. When she left, she gave the woman the quilt as a gift.

Harriet traveled by night, using the North Star as a guide. Both white people and black people helped her along the way. Eventually, she reached Philadelphia. Since many people there were Quakers and against slavery, Philadelphia was a common destination for escaping slaves. When Harriet finally arrived, she said, "I looked at my hands to see if I was the same person. There was such a glory over everything. The sun came out through the trees, and over the fields, and I felt like I was in Heaven." But there was another side to freedom: "There was no one to welcome me to the land of freedom. I was a stranger in a strange land . . ."

Harriet got work as a maid. She was free, but she was also very lonely. So she made a plan.

She'd save her money and return south. She'd help the rest of her family escape. Other slaves, too. In the 1850s, Harriet Tubman led between eleven and nineteen trips.

Harriet's work came to the attention of abolitionists throughout the North. They gave her money to keep going. She became a legend. People said she could see in the dark, sniff danger in the wind, and carry a grown man on her back for miles. These stories were not true, but her fame kept growing.

In 1860, she made her last run as a conductor on the Underground Railroad. It was simply too dangerous for her to continue. Also, the Civil War broke out early in 1861. The Northern states were now fighting against the eleven slave-

WANTED

HARRIET TUBMAN

REWARD

ALSO KNOWN AS 'MOSES'. SHE IS ABOUT 5 FEET TALL AND WEIGHS ABOUT 160 POUNDS. 30 YEARS OLD

holding Southern states that had broken away from the Union. They called their new country the Confederate States of America. Slavery would always remain legal there.

Now Harriet joined the war effort for the North. She became a nurse, tending to black soldiers and hundreds of runaway slaves who poured into Union Army camps.

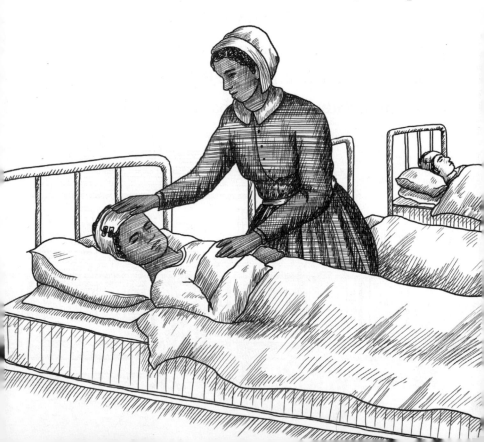

She also worked as a spy behind Southern lines. In early June 1863, she became the first woman to command an army raid. She guided a colonel and his black troops to the Combahee River in South Carolina. There they destroyed bridges, railroad tracks, and stockpiles of cotton, food, and weapons. They also freed over seven hundred slaves.

After the North won the war, slavery finally came to an end. Happily, there was no more need for the Underground Railroad. So its most famous conductor went back to the home she

had bought in Auburn, New York. Harriet was especially proud of the Harriet Tubman Home for the Aged, a place where poor elderly black people could live. It was on land right next to her house in Auburn.

On March 10, 1913, Harriet Tubman died. She was over ninety and had led three hundred people to freedom. She once told a crowd: "I was the conductor of the Underground Railroad for eight years, and can say what most conductors can't say. I never ran my train off the track, and I never lost a passenger."

CHAPTER 6
Special Delivery

Harriet Tubman's name is found in almost every book about American history. Other slaves who escaped the South are not as famous, but their stories of courage are just as important.

Henry Brown was a slave who lived with his mother, sisters, and brothers in the Big House on a plantation in Virginia. His master was not cruel. But in 1830, the master gave Henry away to his son. Henry was only fifteen. Now he lived in another town in Virginia. How he missed his family. Still, he worked hard for his new master. If he didn't, he would be beaten.

A few years later, Henry met and fell in love with a slave named Nancy. She belonged to a different master. Both her master and Henry's

master agreed to let them get married. Henry and Nancy were allowed to live together, and in time they had three children. They felt lucky—until Nancy's master lost a lot of money. Henry was worried. What if Nancy's master sold her and their children?

Sadly, that is exactly what happened. Henry

watched his wife and children being led away. They were going to a new master in North Carolina. Henry knew he would never see them again. He felt like his heart had broken in two.

For weeks, Henry was numb with grief. Things like this could happen because he and his family were slaves. He refused to be a slave any longer.

He had to be free—to be able to go where he wanted and do what he wanted. But how?

Henry thought about it and came up with an unusual idea. He would climb into a large wooden box. He would have someone he trusted "mail" him to an address in Philadelphia. When he stepped out of the box, he'd be free!

First he ordered the box. It was two feet eight inches deep. It was two feet wide. And it was three feet long. Henry wouldn't have much space inside it. The box was lined with a soft green fabric. That would make the trip a little more comfortable. He would carry a small bag of water and some biscuits. Holes in the box let in enough air. Henry spent eighty-six dollars, about half of all the money he had, to pay for the shipping.

So many things could go wrong. Henry could be hurt or crushed in the box. He could be discovered. Then he would be sent back and punished. But Henry was determined.

A friend of Henry's was a white abolitionist

named Samuel A. Smith. He agreed to help mail Henry. Next, Henry needed an excuse to stay home from work. He got hold of a bottle of strong acid used for cleaning metal. Henry poured the acid on his hand! He burned his skin to the bone! It hurt horribly. But now he had a reason to stay home from work. Smith, who was a doctor, bandaged Henry's hand. They agreed to meet the next morning, March 23, 1849, at 4:00 a.m.

Early the next morning, Henry met up with Dr. Smith. It was still dark out. Henry climbed into the box, and it was nailed shut. The box was going to be sent to another abolitionist, William H. Johnson, who lived on Arch Street in Philadelphia. On the top of the box was written THIS SIDE UP WITH CARE. Henry's box traveled north by wagon, railroad, steamboat, and ferry. At one point, he landed upside down! He also could hear the sound of the waves. That meant he had to be on a ship, a ship going to Washington, DC.

Being stuffed inside the box was terrible. Blood rushed to Henry's head. His face felt hot. His eyes hurt. What if his head burst open? But he did not move or make a sound.

At last the box was delivered to the office in Philadelphia. Four men, all abolitionists, were there to greet it. One man tapped on the box. "All right?" he asked. "All right, sir!" was Henry's reply from inside. The men used a saw and hatchet to cut open the box. Out stepped Henry. He had been traveling for twenty-six hours.

He was so happy to be free, he sang a hymn from the Bible.

Henry was given clothing and food. Then he took a walk outside in the fresh air. How good that air must have felt. Later, Henry became a speaker for the Anti-Slavery Society. He was given the nickname "Box," and from then on he always called himself Henry "Box" Brown. He wrote his story. It was published first in Boston in 1849, and again in Manchester, England, in 1851.

When the Fugitive Slave Act of 1850 was passed, Henry fled to England. He was 100 percent safe there. He continued to speak out against slavery in his new country. He married a white woman and began a new family. In 1875, he came back to America with a family magic act. No one knows where or when he died. But his brave and daring escape became part of the history of the Underground Railroad.

Fugitive Slave Act of 1850

Congress passed the Fugitive Slave Act in 1850. If runaway slaves were caught in any state, North or South, they had to be returned to their masters. Abolitionists called it the "Bloodhound Law" because of the dogs that tracked down escaping slaves. These slaves could not ask for a jury trial or to speak on their own behalf. In addition, any person aiding a runaway slave could be put in jail for six months and fined heavily. Law officers who captured a runaway slave were entitled to a bonus or promotion.

Henry Brown was a grown man when he sent himself to freedom. But many runaway slaves were very young, hardly more than children. Here is Caroline Quarlls's story.

On July 4, 1842, everyone in St. Louis, Missouri, was celebrating Independence Day. There were picnics and parades all over town. But sixteen-year-old Caroline Quarlls was too busy to join the fun. Caroline took all the money she had and a box of clothes. She was headed for the Mississippi River. She was running to freedom.

The streets were crowded. She had to avoid horses and people on her way to the docks. Caroline tried to blend in with the crowd. With her light skin and hair, she hoped to pass for white.

At the docks, she saw many riverboats on the busy river. Caroline paid a few dollars for a ticket on one. It took her across the river to the free state of Illinois.

There she rode in a stagecoach to the very last stop on the stagecoach line. She ended up in Milwaukee, Wisconsin. She was now four hundred miles away from her master, Charles Hall. She believed she was safe.

Milwaukee was home to many free blacks and former slaves. Caroline met a barber who seemed nice and offered her a place to stay. Caroline took him up on it. She was scared because even here in Milwaukee there were posters offering a reward for her capture.

Three hundred dollars was a lot of money. Although the barber had been a slave once

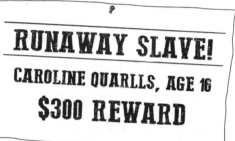

RUNAWAY SLAVE!

CAROLINE QUARLLS, AGE 16

$300 REWARD

himself, he couldn't stop thinking about the money. It would make him a rich man. The barber ended up telling slave catchers where to find Caroline.

Caroline was still hidden in the barber's shack. She did not know what he had done. When she heard a knock on the door, she opened it.

Was it a slave catcher?

No!

There stood Asahel Finch. He was a white man and an abolitionist. He had heard about slave catchers coming after Caroline and wanted to warn her. Caroline fled just in time. A few minutes later, the barber returned with slave catchers.

The slave catchers were furious that Caroline was gone. They gave the barber a beating. Then they went from house to house, looking for the girl. Meanwhile, Caroline and Asahel Finch 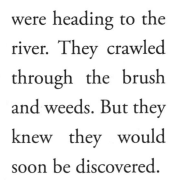 were heading to the river. They crawled through the brush and weeds. But they knew they would soon be discovered.

Caroline and Finch both spotted an old barrel for storing sugar. It was almost covered by weeds. Finch pried off the lid. Caroline jumped inside. Once the barrel was shut, Finch ran off, promising to come back.

For hours, Caroline remained stuffed in the barrel. It was hot, cramped, and dark. Late that night, Caroline heard a voice. Someone was here! Was it a slave catcher? How frightened she must have been. When the lid was pried off, there was Finch again. What a relief!

Finch took Caroline to a safe house, a farm just outside of Milwaukee. Then other conductors took her to another safe house, thirty miles away. It belonged to Samuel and Lucinda Daugherty. Caroline hid there for three weeks.

Meanwhile, the slave catchers hadn't given up looking for her. They set up headquarters in a local tavern. From there, they continued to search. The

slave catchers were sneaky. They told other people
they wanted to *help* Caroline by sending her home,
and that if she gave herself up, they would give her
freedom papers. But these were all lies. Caroline
stayed hidden at the Daughertys' house.

One day, the slave catchers showed up at
the Daughertys'. Caroline ran to the cellar.
The only way out was through a potato chute.
The chute was slippery and narrow. With
her long skirts and petticoat, she barely fit.
But she squeezed in and climbed up it. Once she
was outside, she crawled on her knees through
a cornfield and hid. The slave catchers looked

everywhere but did not find her.
When it was dark, they left.

Caroline was safe,
at least for the
time being.

But she
realized that
she would never
really be free anywhere
in the United States. There
was always the chance of being
caught. She had to get to Canada.
Of course, getting to Canada was not going
to be easy. Most escaped slaves made the trip
by ship, but there were too many slave catchers
looking for her. The docks around Milwaukee

and Kenosha were not safe.

Again, two brave conductors came to Caroline's aid. One was named Lyman Goodnow. He decided to take Caroline to Canada himself. He told people that he was going to "pay the queen a visit." This was code for Canada, which was still ruled by Queen Victoria of England. With a pillowcase of food and a little money, they set off in a horse and wagon with Caroline hidden under hay and a buffalo robe. First, they went south to Illinois, around Chicago. Then they went through Indiana, and up through Michigan.

Along the way they stayed at different stops on the Underground Railroad. Some were very grand houses. Others were tiny shacks. They got wet. They got lost. They were often hungry, and tired. They were always afraid of being caught. But they kept traveling for five hundred miles.

Finally they reached the Detroit River in Michigan. Posters advertising a reward for

Caroline's capture were there, too. Slave catchers roamed the docks. Nevertheless, Caroline managed to cross the river in a ferryboat. When she stepped off on the other side, she was in Sandwich, Canada. Free! She could hardly believe it. She had been on the run from July through October of 1842—four months. She had come more than one thousand miles.

Caroline Quarlls lived in Canada for the rest of her life. She married Allen Watkins and had six children. She learned to read and write.

Years later, in 1880, she wrote these words to her old friend Lyman: *Dearest friend, pen and ink could hardly express my joy when I heard from you*

once more . . . I have never forgotten you nor your
kindness . . . Just as soon as the postmaster read the
name to me—your name—my heart filled with joy
and gladness.

The girl who once hid in a sugar barrel had a sweet ending to her journey on the Underground Railroad.

CHAPTER 8
The Strength of Love

Plantation owners sometimes had children with their own slaves. The babies were born slaves, too. Their father was their master! It was a way for white men to add to the number of slaves they owned without paying any money.

Ellen Craft, born in Clinton, Georgia, was one such slave. She had very light skin because her father was a white plantation owner named Major James Smith. Her mother was a house slave.

Major Smith's wife did not like Ellen, and in 1837, she gave the girl away to her daughter Eliza, who lived in Macon, Georgia. Ellen cried bitterly when she was separated from her mother. She was only eleven. Within a year, Major and Mrs. Smith moved to Macon. That made life better for Ellen.

Now she was able to see her mother sometimes.

Like her mother, Ellen was a house slave. She learned to sew and to speak well. She was such a good worker that her mistress allowed her to live alone in a little cabin behind the Big House.

In time, Ellen met a slave named William Craft. He belonged to another master. When he was younger, William's parents and then his sisters were sold off to different owners. William had not even been allowed to say good-bye.

Because William was a gifted carpenter, his master put him to work in a furniture shop. He also worked in a hotel, waiting on tables. His master took most of his earnings, but William got to keep a small amount. This little bit of money was to become very important in time.

William and Ellen fell in love. Ellen was afraid to marry because she had seen too many slave couples pulled apart and separated for life. But eventually she said yes. She loved William and she wanted children, but not children who would be slaves. Ellen decided there was only one answer: escape. How would they ever do it, though? They lived in Macon, Georgia. That was the Deep South. The closest free states—Ohio and Pennsylvania—were almost eight hundred miles away.

Then William got an idea. With her light skin, Ellen could pass for a white person. And she spoke like her masters. Ellen would pretend to be a gentleman from the South. William would pretend to be her slave. They could travel by train and steamboat to southern Pennsylvania.

William set the plan in motion. He used some of his saved money to buy a top hat.

He also bought a gentleman's coat and boots. Ellen sewed herself a pair of men's pants. Then

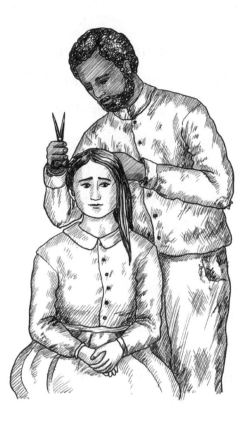

William cut off her hair. But she still looked like a woman. So he bought her dark glasses and tried wrapping a handkerchief around her face. Back then, people often did that when they had a toothache. Yes! This disguise might work. No one could see Ellen's pretty face. With the top hat and new clothes, she looked like a man.

Christmas was coming. Ellen's mistress gave Ellen permission to visit relatives. William's owner did the same. So now they had a whole week away from their owners. It would be seven days before anyone came looking for them. By that time, they hoped to be in Pennsylvania. There was just one more problem: Ellen could not write. What if someone asked the "gentleman" to sign his name on a ticket? They thought about this for days. Then Ellen got the idea to bind her arm in a sling. A broken arm was the perfect excuse for not being able to write.

Four days before the Christmas of 1848, William and Ellen set out at dawn.

At every turn on the long trip, they ran into trouble. First it was at the train station.

They did not know that William's boss at the furniture store was suspicious and had come looking for him. He ran along the platform, peering in every window of the train. Ellen, in disguise, was in the car for whites. But William was in the car for blacks. Just as the store owner reached it, the conductor rang the bell. Away went the train. The Crafts were safe—but only for the moment.

In the car for whites, a man sat down next to Ellen. Oh no! He was a friend of her owners.

Ellen had met him many times. She was terrified that he would recognize her. When he spoke to her, she pretended she couldn't hear. Imagine her relief when he got off the train a few stops later.

By early evening, the train arrived in Savannah, Georgia. The Crafts got off and took a carriage to the waterfront, where they got on board a steamboat bound for Charleston, South Carolina. Ellen called herself "Mr. Johnson." William was her slave. Because she was pretending to be white, Ellen was given a cabin while William had to stay on the deck all night. He grabbed a couple of hours sleep on some bags of cotton near the boat's funnel. By morning, he was exhausted and weak from hunger.

Mr. Johnson let his slave come to the table for breakfast and gave him scraps from his plate. Some of the other passengers did not approve of this. They told Mr. Johnson he was "spoiling" his slave. That made Ellen so angry, but she could not show it.

Another scare came when they arrived in Charleston, South Carolina. While Ellen tried to buy two tickets for the steamboat and the train to Philadelphia, a ticket seller asked William if he belonged to Mr. Johnson. William said yes, but the ticket seller insisted Mr. Johnson sign his name on a ledger book to prove it. Mr. Johnson pointed to his arm, but the ticket seller just told him to use his other hand.

The Crafts were terrified. What was Ellen going to do now?

Fortunately, one of the passengers they had met while on the steamboat to Charleston showed up.

He said he knew Mr. Johnson, and was willing to vouch for him. Once more, the Crafts were on their way. They went by steamboat up the coast to Wilmington, North Carolina.

In Wilmington, they got off the boat and changed to another train. Their troubles were not over. On the train, a woman mistook William for her escaped slave. After discovering her mistake, she apologized but kept on gabbing about how she'd sold off the runaway slave's wife. That's why he had run away—to find his wife. When Mr. Johnson muttered that the woman had been "unkind," the woman grew very angry.

Other passengers turned to listen to the argument. Once more, Ellen was terrified. She had to keep her temper—she had to! She did not say one more word, but let the woman rant about ungrateful slaves who ran away.

Ellen and William got off the train near Fredericksburg, Virginia. Next they went by steamboat up the Potomac River to Washington, DC. It was Christmas Eve. From Washington, the Crafts caught a train to Baltimore, Maryland. After that, there was only one more train— the one that would take them to Pennsylvania. While still in Baltimore, they had to deal with a stationmaster who wanted to see papers proving that Mr. Johnson owned William. Of course, Ellen did not have any such papers. But she stayed calm and stated firmly that she had bought the tickets and intended to remain on the train. Her firm manner worked. The stationmaster let them on.

Ellen and William each went to their separate

cars. They were both exhausted and fell asleep immediately. On Christmas Day, they woke up in Pennsylvania—free at last!

Of course, by now their masters realized they had run away. Slave hunters would be on the lookout for them. They had to be very careful. Abolitionists in Pennsylvania sent them much farther north to Boston. Ellen found work sewing. William opened a shop where he made cabinets and sold used furniture. They made friends with a former slave named William Wells Brown. He took them on a lecture tour, and they told their story. They became well known among abolitionists.

Even in Boston they were not safe. One day, a white man named John Knight showed up. He was from the furniture shop where William had worked in Macon, Georgia. Knight was traveling with another man named Hughes. These two men had been sent by William's former owner to catch them. Knight and Hughes hung around the Crafts' apartment and shop, waiting for them.

But hundreds of Bostonians, both black and white, rallied around the Crafts. They knew them from the lecture tour. These new friends guarded the Crafts' home and threatened the slave catchers.

Knight and Hughes went back to Macon empty-handed. Ellen and William were grateful for the support. But like Henry "Box" Brown, they decided to move to England. There they would be beyond the reach of slave catchers. Before they left the United States, they did something they had wanted to do for a long time. On November 7, 1850, they went to a minister, who married them.

Slave hunters patrolled the docks in Boston, so instead of trying to sail straight to England, they went by stagecoach to Halifax, on the coast of Canada. They planned to board a ship from there.

However, nothing went easily for the Crafts. Near Halifax, the stagecoach overturned in a violent storm.

Ellen and William had to walk the last seven miles to the city in the pouring rain. They managed to book passage on a ship. But Ellen came down with pneumonia. Back then there were no antibiotics to stop a disease like pneumonia. Several times on the trip across the Atlantic Ocean, it looked like she would die. But she hung on and got well again. A few days before Christmas in 1850, they saw the coast of England before them. It had been almost two years since they had left Georgia for freedom.

Life in England was good. The Crafts went to school, ran a boardinghouse, and wrote a book about their long and difficult journey. They bought a house outside London and raised a family. Their daughter, four sons, and three adopted sons from Africa fulfilled Ellen's dream: The Crafts had children and they were all free.

After the Civil War, the Crafts went back to Georgia. They settled in Savannah, where they opened a school for poor people. They helped care for sick neighbors and even paid for the weddings of young black couples. After all, it was the Crafts' strong and enduring love that had helped them deal with so many dangers on the road to freedom.

CHAPTER 9
Changed

At the end of the Civil War, in 1865, slavery was abolished in the United States. But black people soon found that being free did not mean that they were treated the same way that white people were. Even a hundred years later, African Americans were not seen as equal and did not have the same rights as whites. This was especially true in the South, where the two races lived separately.

This way of life was called segregation. (To *segregate* people means to keep them apart.)

Blacks were not allowed to buy houses in white neighborhoods. They were not allowed to attend white schools, eat in white restaurants, stay at white hotels, or go to white laundromats. Signs outside said, FOR WHITES ONLY.

Then in the 1950s and 1960s, great changes came through the civil rights movement.

African Americans united in their demand for equality, under leaders such as Martin Luther King Jr. Just like slavery had been outlawed a century earlier, segregation was now made illegal.

A milestone came in 1965 with the Voting Rights Act. It guaranteed African Americans the right to cast votes, and thus elect leaders who would represent their interests and rights.

Martin Luther King Jr.

Martin Luther King Jr. was born on January 15, 1929, in Atlanta, Georgia. The son of a minister, King became a minister and civil-rights activist. Through marches and peaceful protests, he helped end segregation in the South. He gave his famous "I Have a Dream" speech in August 1963 at a huge march in Washington, DC.

King's dream was for a country where blacks and whites lived together as equals. Here is a well-known line from it: *"I have a dream that my four little children will one day live in a nation where they will not be judged by the color of their skin but by the content of their character."* On April 4, 1968, he was shot and killed in Memphis, Tennessee. He is still remembered as one of the greatest African American leaders in history.

Will prejudice against black people *ever* disappear completely? That is a question that can't really be answered. Runaway slaves didn't think about being treated the same way as white people. All they wanted was to be free. Could Henry "Box" Brown or Harriet Tubman ever have imagined that in 2008 a black man would be elected president of the United States?

Or that he would have a wife whose ancestors had once been slaves in the Deep South?

Change may often seem to come too slowly, but in time it does come.

Timeline of the Underground Railroad

1619	About twenty people kidnapped from West Africa are sold in Jamestown, Virginia, as North America's first slaves
1777	Vermont becomes the first North American colony to abolish slavery
1808	The US bans the slave trade, but some African slaves are still smuggled into the country
1831	In Boston, William Lloyd Garrison founds an abolitionist newspaper called the *Liberator*
	A slave named Nat Turner leads a rebellion in Southampton, Virginia, during which at least fifty-five white people are killed
	Tice Davids, a slave, flees from Kentucky to Ohio
1842	On Independence Day, sixteen-year-old Caroline Quarlls crosses the Mississippi River into the free state of Illinois
1848	Ellen and William Craft escape to the North by pretending to be a master and his slave
1849	Harriet Tubman escapes to freedom
	Henry Brown travels to Philadelphia in a box and emerges as a freeman
1861	Eleven Southern states secede and form the Confederate States of America

Timeline of the World

The Pilgrims on the *Mayflower* land in Plymouth, Massachusetts	1620
Between 75,000 and 100,000 people in London die from the Great Plague	1665
The first encyclopedia is published	1751
The Declaration of Independence is signed in Philadelphia, Pennsylvania	1776
The Revolutionary War ends	1783
Eli Whitney invents the cotton gin	1793
The War of 1812 begins	1812
Civil rights leader Frederick Douglass is born a slave in Tuckahoe, Maryland	1818
Mexico gains independence from Spain	1821
Slavery is abolished in the British Empire	1833
Victoria becomes the queen of Great Britain	1837
Uncle Tom's Cabin by Harriet Beecher Stowe becomes a best seller	1852
The Civil War is fought; the North wins	1861–5
Louis Pasteur invents pasteurization	1864
The Thirteenth Amendment to the US Constitution ends slavery nationwide	1865

Bibliography

*Books for young readers

*Bial, Raymond. *The Underground Railroad*. New York: Houghton Mifflin, 1995.

Bordewich, Fergus M. *Bound for Canaan: The Underground Railroad and the War for the Soul of America*. New York: Amistad, 2005.

*Dennis, Denise. *Black History for Beginners*. New York: Writers and Readers, 1984.

DeRamus, Betty. *Freedom by Any Means*. New York: Atria, 2009.

*Fradin, Dennis Brindell. *The Underground Railroad*. New York: Marshall Cavendish Benchmark, 2012.

*——. *Bound for the North Star: True Stories of Fugitive Slaves*. New York: Clarion Books, 2000.

*Levine, Ellen. *Henry's Freedom Box: A True Story from the Underground Railroad*. New York: Scholastic Press, 2007.

*McDonough, Yona Zeldis. *Who Was Harriet Tubman?* New York: Grosset and Dunlap, 2002.

*Osborne, Linda Barrett. *Travelling the Freedom Road: From Slavery & the Civil War through Reconstruction*. New York: Abrams, 2009.

*Pferdehirt, Julia. *Freedom Train North: Stories of the Underground Railroad in Wisconsin*. Wisconsin Historical Society Press, 2011.

*Raatma, Lucia. *The Underground Railroad*. New York: Children's Press, 2012.

*Stein, R. Conrad. *Escaping Slavery on the Underground Railroad*. Enslow: Berkeley Heights, NJ, 2008.

Still, William. *The Underground Railroad: A Record of Facts . . .* Philadelphia: Porter & Coates, 1872. Reprinted as *The Underground Railroad: Authentic Narratives and First Hand Accounts*. New York: Dover Publications, 2007.

*Waxman, Laura Hamilton. *How Did Slaves Find a Route to Freedom?: And Other Questions About the Underground Railroad*. Minneapolis: Lerner, 2011.